MIST OVER THE MOUNTAINS

Appalachia and Its People

MIST OVER THE MOUNTAINS

Appalachia and Its People

Raymond Bial

Houghton Mifflin Company
Boston 1997

Acknowledgments

This book would not have been possible without the generous help of a number of individuals and organizations who have dedicated themselves to preserving the culture of Appalachia. I would especially like to thank Ed Ford and Claude Hammond of Berea College for steering me in the right direction and helping to locate key photographs. I am deeply indebted to John Rice Irwin for allowing me to photograph at the Museum of Appalachia and for contributing a number of photographs for *Mist Over the Mountains*. I would also like to express my appreciation to the staff of the Museum of Appalachia for their gracious assistance.

I would like to thank the National Archives for making available a number of photographs by Russell Lee, and Eric G. Ackerman for providing several wonderful photographs from the Earl Palmer Collection, Special Collections Department / University Libraries, Virginia Polytechnic Institute and State University.

I am indebted as well to Earl Palmer, Warren Brunner, and Russell Lee, who generously contributed their best work, and to Genell Fisk, who provided some delightful family stories for this book. As always, my editor, Audrey Bryant, deserves high praise for transforming a weighty manuscript and an abundance of photographs into a meaningful book.

Most importantly, I would like to thank once again my wife, Linda, and my children, Anna, Sarah, and Luke, for their sweet inspiration.

The text of this book is set in 14 point Goudy.

Manufactured in Singapore
TWP 10 9 8 7 6 5 4 3 2 1

Library of Congress Cataloging-in-Publication Data

Bial, Raymond.
    Mist over the mountains : Appalachia and its people / by Raymond Bial.
    p. cm.
    Summary: An overview of life past and present in the geographic region known as Appalachia.
    ISBN 0-395-73569-6
1. Mountain whites (Southern States) — Social life and customs — Juvenile literature.
2. Mountain whites (Southern States — History — Juvenile literature. 3. Appalachian Region, Southern — Juvenile literature. [1. Appalachian Region. 2. Mountain life — Appalachian Region.]   I. Title
F217.A65B53 1997
975 — dc20   96-7466
CIP AC

This book is respectfully dedicated to all the wonderful people who have devoted themselves to sustaining the folk culture of Appalachia and helping others understand the spirit of the mountains.

From the valleys to the mountain peaks, much of Appalachia is blanketed with sprawling forests. At higher elevations, the ranges of mountains may be softened by low-hanging clouds, which lend a sense of mystery to the region.

The word "Appalachia" brings many images to mind. "Most people don't know if it's a state or what—or even where it is," says Emily Wallace, who was born and raised in the mountains of eastern Tennessee. "Appalachia is not just a place but a culture."

As a place, Appalachia is a chain of mountain ranges that begins in northern Alabama and stretches all the way north to Newfoundland in Canada. The ranges include the Blue Ridge Mountains, the Great Smoky Mountains, the Allegheny Mountains,

Born and raised in Appalachia, Emily Wallace and Anna Tuberville appreciate tradition, but the two college students also like to go to movies and hang out with their friends.

Laced with rivers and streams, the mountains and valleys of Appalachia are the oldest in the United States. Over thousands of years, ancient streambeds have cut deeply into the hillsides as the water tumbled over rocks and fallen trees.

the Cumberland Plateau, and the Great Valley, which lies west of the Blue Ridge, but it's the mountain areas of Georgia, Tennessee, Kentucky, Virginia, West Virginia, North Carolina, and Maryland that are generally regarded as Appalachia.

Appalachia is undeniably lovely. The landscape alternates between pleasant green coves, or valleys, and mountains softened by trees. White clouds hover over the peaks, which offer grand views from high above the valleys. It's easy to see why the area is known for its natural beauty—Appalachia is one of the most scenic places in North America. And although some areas have been strip-mined for coal or clear-cut for lumber, much of the land remains as it was thousands of years ago—slopes of hardy timber interlaced with streams that splash over rocks and sparkle beneath roofs of green leaves.

The culture of Appalachia, however, is often misunderstood. "Most people don't know anything about Appalachia," Emily Wallace contends. "They come in here and ask me, 'Do you have an outhouse?' They think we all go around barefoot."

Misconceptions about Appalachia are partly due to the region's isolation. In the past, the mountains

When white settlers began to arrive in the mountains, the Cherokee traded with them and adopted European dress, metal tools such as the ax, and practices such as the use of log cabins.

With sunlight splashing through the branches, the canopy of towering trees provided a sense of shelter against wind and weather as settlers made their way high into the mountains.

were not only beautiful but also an effective barrier against the outside world. Rising from the southern flatlands, they afforded early settlers both protection and isolation, which over time shaped the character of the people who lived there. Those people needed to be both self-reliant and able to depend on each other to survive in often unpredictable and inhospitable surroundings.

From the outside, the people of Appalachia have often been viewed as either fiercely independent pioneer stock or backward hillbillies. The term "hillbilly" first appeared in print in 1900 in the *New York Journal*, which defined a hillbilly as "a free and untrammeled white citizen of Alabama, who lives in the hills, has no means to speak of, dresses as he can, talks as he pleases, drinks whiskey when he gets it, and fires off his revolver as the fancy takes him." Humorous depictions followed in comic strips with such characters as Snuffy Smith and L'il Abner. Others, such as Aaron Copland, who composed the ballet *Appalachian Spring*, have evoked a lovely region and a proud, intelligent people.

In reality, Appalachians are no better or worse than other people in America and around the world. Yet they do have distinctive features that help define the character of the region. Tradition and culture are especially important to Appalachians, and the beginnings of their folkways can be traced back to the Cherokee Indians and the first European settlers. The history of these early inhabitants is an important key to understanding the people who live in the region today.

The first Appalachians were the Cherokee, who lived in the mountains hundreds of years before Columbus arrived in North America. A woodland tribe, they farmed, hunted, and gathered wild plants and berries. Their society was based on a system of clans, with women heading households.

In the 1700s, well before the American Revolution, the first people of European descent made their way into the region. Gradually, Pennsylvanians moved southward along the limestone valleys of the

White settlers adopted many Cherokee farming practices, such as hanging rows of gourd birdhouses near vegetable gardens. The birdhouses attract martins, which devour enormous numbers of insects.

Blue Ridge, Virginians migrated up the Potomac and James rivers, and settlers from the Carolinas traveled the Wilderness Road and the Little Tennessee River to new homes in Appalachia. Mostly English, Scotch-Irish, and German, many of these people were poor, and they entered the mountains to begin life on their own farms. Even if it meant eking out a meager living on the rocky slopes, they would at least own a piece of land for the first time in their lives. They longed to be independent and finally to provide for themselves.

In the beginning, Native Americans and the new settlers coexisted peacefully. But as competition for land intensified, a series of fierce battles took place, culminating in the forcible removal of the Cherokee to an Oklahoma reservation in 1838. Men, women, and children were compelled to march westward an incredible 700 miles without adequate food, clothing, or shelter. Fully one quarter of the 16,000 Cherokee died of starvation, disease, exposure to the weather, or mistreatment by soldiers on the now infamous "Trail of Tears." Descendents of the survivors, known as the Western Cherokee, still live in Oklahoma. However, many Cherokee refused to leave the Appalachians and disappeared into the mountains, where they eluded the invading soldiers. Today their descendants, the Eastern Cherokee, flourish 10,000 strong on tribal land in western North Carolina.

Sturdy fences were essential on wilderness homesteads. The sharp pickets on this fence protected cornfields and gardens from both free-ranging livestock and wild animals.

Like the Cherokee before them, the new settlers in Appalachia had to become self-reliant if they were going to survive in a land that was still very much wilderness. It wasn't an easy life. A pioneer woman known as Aunt Liza recalled her youth in the late 1800s: "There's snakes, of course, rattlers, out on the ridge, but they don't come about the place now like they used to. There was bears here, too, when we first come; they used to get our hogs and young calves. My old man always took his gun with him whenever he'd go off anywheres from the house."

Before roads offered access, it was extremely difficult for settlers to work their way through the steep hills and rocky valleys in wagons pulled by

teams of oxen or horses. Even foot travel was hard in the mountains. "When I was little, there were no roads up here, only branch beds with water running down them," recalled Levie Greene Odom. "My daddy, he always kept a team and wagon. He'd haul his apples and taters to Johnson City to peddle. It would take three days."

Settlers from the 1700s all the way to the late 1800s were almost all subsistence farmers, which means that their farms provided nearly everything

Even after hundreds of years of settlement, in many areas of Appalachia forest still stretches mile upon mile, untouched by encroaching roads.

Living deep in the woods, far from any stores, settlers had to provide for themselves. Most brought useful skills with them, including the ability to farm and build log cabins.

the family needed to survive but very little to spare. It was a difficult existence requiring hard work and skill to get by. Howard Burleson, who has lived his entire life along Greasy Creek in the mountains of North Carolina, remembers, "We'd have to buy coffee, salt, sugar, and flour. Everything else we raised ourselves."

"What we couldn't raise or make, we learned to live without," echoes Dewey Ingram, who grew up high in the mountains of North Carolina.

One of the most important buildings on the farm was the family home, usually a log cabin built by the settlers themselves. Cabins were made from trees felled by farmers, and designs had colorful names: single pen, dogtrot (also called possum trot), or saddlebag. The single pen was just that, a single room. The dogtrot had an open hallway between the two halves of the house, while the saddlebag consisted of two rooms with a central chimney and two front doors. Though log cabins are found in other places, they remain a strong symbol of the heritage of independence in the mountains. Some Appalachians still live in log cabins, and the rugged buildings are highly valued.

Farmers typically planted corn, wheat, and hay as feed for livestock—chickens, sheep, hogs, and per-

Appalachian settlers slept in one- or two-room cabins that were often drafty. Through the long winter nights, folks kept warm under layers of carefully stitched handmade quilts.

With no grocery stores in the mountains, settlers grew and preserved their harvest for the winter. Canning is still practiced in many parts of the mountains.

haps a milk cow. Sorghum and tobacco were also grown as cash crops—crops sold for money. Tobacco was especially important, because even though the crop had to be painstakingly tended by hand, it could be profitably grown on farms with small acreages. Sorghum canes were harvested for their juice, which was boiled down into a syrup sold for cash and used as a sweetener on the home table.

Large vegetable gardens were always necessary on mountain farms, with most of the harvest stored for the winter in root cellars. Dug into the side of a hill, lined with logs or rocks, and covered with a roof, these small underground rooms kept a constant temperature. Safe canning methods were developed around 1825, and over the course of the next hundred years Mason jars gradually replaced root cellars.

In many remote areas, the pioneer way of life continued well into the 1920s. People still farmed small parcels of land and lived in the log buildings constructed by their ancestors, with outhouses in back. The persistence of early ways up to modern times may be where the stereotype of backward Appalachians began, but some of these people chose to live in a traditional manner. They enjoyed the mountains and didn't want any part of modern life. As contemporary author Janice Holt Giles explained on her move to the mountains, "We have created a very complex civilization, fast-moving,

Large, extended families still frequently spend time together, as at this reunion of the Elmo Adams family held in Floyds Branch, Kentucky. (Courtesy Warren Brunner)

Men and mules often worked together plowing, planting, and cultivating mountain fields and gardens. Today, some farmers still depend on mules to work their fields. (Above: courtesy the Museum of Appalachia. Opposite: courtesy Warren Brunner.)

noisy, crowded, and nervous, in which we are not entirely at home. It has come too fast and our personalities cannot adjust to it fully. Most of us remember, or at least our parents can remember, a slower day, a quieter day, and in our memories perhaps, a sweeter day."

Well into the twentieth century many people in Appalachia continued to get by on small homesteads, eking out a living with horses or mules—and some still do. "I've plowed just about every foot of this land with a team of horses, so I know what it is," said Garlan Hughes, of Buladean, North Carolina. "It will grow anything you want in the vegetable

Silhouetted against the mountain sky and set off from the forest by a picket fence, this old cabin has endured for more than a century. Log cabins embody the spirit of Appalachia; they stand as a strong, clear symbol of people's respect for their ancestors and the past.

line—potatoes, corn, tomatoes, peppers, strawberries, canteloupes. And of course it grows tobacco."

To this day, some Appalachians prefer the old ways of farming. "Nothing tickles me better than to get a couple of horses and go to plowing," says Howard Burleson. "But it *is* hard work." Although mules can at times be difficult, they are preferred for working mountain farms because they are surefooted on slopes and can do more work on less feed than horses or oxen. Before tractors were invented, mules were essential to small farms, and at the mule-power peak in 1925, four and a half million of the long-eared beasts were working in the South. In the mountains, farmers relied primarily on mules well into the 1950s, long after tractors were common.

Many couldn't afford the machines, and tractors couldn't be used on steep hillsides.

Plowing, planting, and harvesting, Appalachians struggled foot by foot to get by on their small farms. They came to love the land for which they had fought so hard, and today Appalachians remain deeply attached to their homes, whether small frame houses in the valley or mountain cabins. Many homes have been handed down for generations, fostering a strong connection both to the land and to family. Maye Buchanan Tipton's recollection is typical: "When my dad died, he said, 'I want anybody in

Photographs of family members, including grandparents, cousins, aunts, and uncles often adorned the log walls of early cabins in Appalachia, as they do in homes today.

In the homes scattered throughout the mountains, family members often gathered around the dinner table for good food and lively conversation. In the evenings, they sat out on the porches and told stories, perhaps a Jack tale or the story of their grand-parents' courtship.

the family to be able to come back here as long as there is any Buchanan alive.'"

Along with this attachment comes a powerful sense of kinship. Not only are brothers and sisters, parents and grandparents close, but cousins and aunts and uncles all know each other. In the beginning, families needed to stick together to survive in what was often a hardscrabble existence, and the feeling frequently endures today. Even when relatives aren't of the finest character, they're still family. Two men discussing their cousin concluded he wasn't exactly a good man, "but he's our'n."

In the past, people relied on family and often viewed others with suspicion—not just "flatlanders," but other mountain families, as evidenced by the infamous feud between the Hatfields and the McCoys. Strong clan loyalties, mixed with moonshine, led to many bloody disputes between these two families over seemingly minor issues, including the ownership of a razorback hog. During the course of the feud, which lasted from the Civil War to 1897, when one Hatfield was hanged and several others were sent to prison, there were numerous gun battles and a romance between "Devil Anse" Hatfield's son and a McCoy daughter. Today, some Appalachians remain clannish and shy away from outsiders; others are friendly and outgoing.

Obviously, Appalachians have been known to live by their own rules at times. Moonshining, the distilling of homemade whiskey, is perhaps the best-known case of people clashing with the government. When the Eighteenth Amendment to the Constitution was passed in 1919, making it illegal to sell, manufacture, import, or export liquor, moonshiners set up hidden stills in the woods to make their own. Although more than a few jokes have been made about "corn juice" (also called panther's breath, rotgut, ruckus juice, tiger's sweat, and white lightning), making the clear, raw liquor was—and still is—considered an acceptable practice in the mountains, as well as an example of ingenuity. Moon-

shiner Aaron Goad recalled that in the 1920s and 1930s every adult in Floyd County, Virginia, "drank it, made it, sold it, or run it." On their small farms, mountain folk could rarely grow enough corn as a cash crop to make a living. Bartering only got them a due bill at the local store, but if they used a small amount of corn for moonshine, it could bring in a little extra income. A bottle of 'shine could get enough money to buy your child a pair of shoes or

Moonshine was made by cooking a corn mash over a carefully tended fire at a secret place in the woods. Although stills were well hidden, revenuers sometimes located them by watching for the smoke rising through the trees. (Courtesy the Earl Palmer Collection, Virginia Polytechnic Institute and State University)

overalls. Although the making of home brew was illegal, Goad states, "I never give the sheriff any trouble, 'cept in catching me, but when I was caught, I was his'n." Moonshine is still made in some isolated parts of the mountains, even in "dry" counties, where the sale of alcoholic beverages is forbidden.

Religion is also vitally important to mountain people. Media accounts have sensationalized unusual expressions of faith, such as snake handling, and roadside signs reminding motorists that "Jesus Saves" and "Christ is the Answer," or cautioning "Repent or Perish," are familiar sights. Revivals are common in the mountains, as are full-immersion baptisms in the local creek. However, a white frame country church nestled in a valley offers a more typical symbol of beliefs in the region. There are a number of denominations in the mountains, but Baptists and Methodists have by far the largest membership. In keeping with the fiery independence of mountain people, churches are not strongly allied with larger national organizations, such as the Southern Baptist Conference, and many Appalachians are not affiliated with any denomination or follow a variant such as the Free Will Baptists. Most mountaineers are religious, but not churchgoers; less than half the population regularly attends services. Favoring that "old-time religion," those who do go prefer traditional services, and the sounds of hymns such as

"Rock of Ages" and "The Old Rugged Cross" rise out of the valleys on Sundays. Some groups are very strict; they don't hold with dancing, women wearing pants, or even playing musical instruments.

Historically, the church has stood at the very center of the community, although it is now in decline. Recalling the 163 quarts of apple butter she once made for a church function, Geneva Hughes said, "It was worth it just to bring everyone together like that. Why, used to be people'd come together for

People attend small country churches scattered among the hills and hollows. Members of the congregation often construct and maintain the church buildings themselves.

Dulcimers like this fine instrument made by Jacob Michael Neff are still lovingly crafted by mountain artisans. The inscription on the back reads, "J. M. Neff April 20, 1890. It is raining today."

bean stringin's, quilt makin's, apple butter. Just nobody has time anymore."

Religion, along with an Old World heritage, has also deeply influenced Appalachian music. The music has a country flavor; twangy vocals are accompanied by string instruments, usually guitar, banjo, fiddle, and the less familiar dulcimer. The dulcimer, based on European instruments and refined in Pennsylvania, appeared in Appalachia only in the mid-1800s, but today it is closely identified with the region. It's played on the lap by plucking strings, and its soft, sweet, sometimes melancholy sound reflects the atmosphere of the mountains.

The fiddle is a key instrument for square dancing and clog dancing. Clog dancing is a combination of square dancing and the "buck dance," a one-person dance similar to an Irish jig. It's thought that clogging got its start in western North Carolina in the 1920s, and it's still popular in many places today.

Another tradition that has held an especially important place in Appalachian homes is storytelling. "I grew up in a family of incredible talkers,

Fiddles were also made by Appalachian craftsmen. Here, John Rice Irwin plays a fiddle crafted by A. L. "Fate" Cassidy in 1910. Cassidy fiddles are considered exceptional instruments and are very rare.

Often cash-poor, mountain folk have had to improvise, even in making musical instruments. When Dan Pugh decided he wanted a banjo, he made one with materials at hand— in this case, a Selecto ham can.

and I myself am an incredible talker," says eastern Kentucky author Gurney Norman. Mountain people are known for their ability to preach and tell stories. The flavor of the language— sayings, place names,

and ways of speaking—reflects the character of the people and their way of life.

"Settin' out" on the porch of an evening, storytellers might recount a classic, such as one of the Jack tales, a group of stories that originated in Britain and were enhanced in the mountains of North Carolina. In almost every tale, Jack exhibits courage, skill, and intelligence—all traits valued in the mountains—to outwit his adversary as he struggles to free his family from poverty.

Also popular are tall tales (also called windies, whoppers, or simply lies) and ghost stories. Or sto-

When photographer Earl Palmer stopped by Evie Shelton's store in Floyd County, Virginia, in 1955, storytellers had gathered to spin a few yarns of the old days. People still meet in local stores to catch up on events and swap stories. (Courtesy the Earl Palmer Collection, Virginia Polytechnic Institute and State University.)

Mountain men were often handy with tools, including a whittling knife. Coal miner Troy Webb, who lives "straight up" the side of a mountain in Tennessee, has been making dolls like these since the 1940s.

When his children grew up and left home, Andrew Gennet "Papa Jack" Weems took up carving to amuse himself and visitors. He made this African American limber jack, or dancing man, in the 1930s.

ries may come from life. Personal or family stories tell of births, courtships, and other major events in life. Personal knowledge is especially valued: it's said that "when an old person dies, a library burns."

Mountain people also became known for folk arts and crafts, from whittling to making elaborate quilts. Whatever the form, natural materials have always been preferred, both because they are readily available and because of the artists' regard for nature. Wood—especially oak, maple, ash, and hickory—is most often used because of its look and feel. The practice of traditional handiwork is also a means of honoring the past, and a craft is usually learned from someone else, often a family member. Most Appalachian art repeats traditional patterns rather than creating original designs, helping to keep the past alive.

In times past wood was fashioned into furniture, utensils, even toys. Some toys, such as the cup-and-

Early Appalachian women couldn't afford to buy whole cloth. Yet they made striking patchwork quilts, usually in traditional designs such as this log cabin pattern, from scraps of fabric salvaged from worn-out clothes.

ball game, originated in Europe. Other wooden toys had unusual names, such as whammydiddles (also called hooey sticks or geegaw whimmydiddles), and dolls were carved from wood. Because of both poverty and self-reliance, Applachians continued to make toys for their children long after others turned to store-bought merchandise. Some woodworkers still make toys today for craft shops.

Appalachian woodworking is known for its simplicity. A mountain woodworker needs only a few tools—axe, knife, pole lathe (a tool used for rounding legs of tables and chairs), and froe (a tool used for splitting logs)—to make a chair. The town craftsman might use an assortment of seventy-five to a hundred different tools.

One traditional Appalachian craft that is thriving today is basketmaking. There are two basic styles. Cherokee baskets are intricate and supple,

while Anglo-American baskets make use of more rigid hardwoods, particularly white oak. Machines simply cannot produce baskets of superior quality, and handmade Appalachian baskets of both styles are highly prized by collectors.

Appalachian people, however, have not always been isolated farmers and craftspeople. In the late 1800s, the railroad finally penetrated the mountains, and, sensing profit, industry followed. This abrupt change dramatically altered both landscape and people. As early as 1884, the West Virginia Tax Commission warned that outsiders were rapidly purchasing land and predicted that the state would

Early pioneers often used white oak baskets, which are still made and sold in craft shops. Linking the past with the present, the baskets embody both strength and beauty in their design.

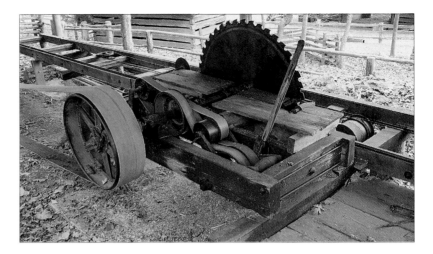

New technology in the late 1800s, this type of saw replaced the two-man handsaw. Set up on a wooded slope, the saw sliced logs into boards as quickly as the logs could be pushed against the large circular blade.

soon "pass into the hands of persons who do not live here and care nothing for our State except to pocket the treasures which lie buried in our hills." The mountains were laid open to these large companies, most of which extracted resources and left nothing.

First came the lumber industry, which provided jobs but also ravaged mountainsides and polluted streams. Until the late 1800s, logging in Appalachia was laborious: trees were felled, the logs dragged over rough hillsides by horses or mules to a stream, then floated to sawmills. After the Civil War, new hand tools made logging faster and easier, and when large machinery was introduced in the region, companies cut down entire forests, leaving mountainsides completely bare. The result is still painfully apparent: entire hillsides have been eroded by runoffs.

But timber wasn't the only exploitable resource in the mountains. The slopes of Appalachia were filled with pockets of gleaming anthracite, a superior

grade of coal. With the industrialization of America in the latter half of the nineteenth century, coal became an essential fuel for trains, factories, and homes. At first men dug coal by hand on the hillsides of their own farms to earn a little extra money. But the industry grew rapidly, and the coalfields of Appalachia eventually reached from Pennsylvania to northern Alabama.

Large numbers of Appalachian farmers were lured into the mines by the prospect of earning cash income, but there were still not enough workers to keep up with the demand. African Americans from

Mining meant long, hard hours in complete darkness. Blackened with coal dust, this exhausted miner from Harlan County, Kentucky, was photographed with his family in 1946 at the end of his shift. (Photo by Russell Lee, courtesy the National Archives)

Appalachian men worked long hours in the mines, but still lived in deep poverty. When the mines closed, they were left even poorer—so poor they could barely put food on the table.

as far away as the Gulf states were brought into the mountains, often in cattle cars, and some of their descendants still live in the mountains today. Only a few African Americans lived in Appalachia during colonial times, but their population grew dramatically after 1870, when they were needed as cheap labor in the mines, though they still make up a very small proportion of the Appalachian population.

Immigrants, primarily from eastern and southern Europe, also moved into the mountains and valleys, often settling in "company towns" built by the coal industry. In these towns, workers became completely dependent on the company, which owned their homes and forced them to pay high prices for food, clothing, and other necessities at the company store. Men could work underground their entire lives and still be in debt to the company. The history of coal production in America is marked by exploitation and bitter labor conflicts, including strikes. The workers struck to protest not only low wages but high accident rates—there were numerous deaths from cave-ins and explosions—and illnesses, such as black lung, caused by unsafe working conditions.

The boom in coal production continued from 1880 to 1930, falling off in the Great Depression and picking up again during World War II. At that time 40 percent of the country's production came from Appalachian coalfields. Once the war was over, however, demand fell. About this time, mining also became more mechanized and fewer workers were needed. In the United States the numbers fell from a high of 862,536 miners in 1923 to barely 100,000 miners today. Suddenly unemployed, many Appalachians in the 1950s, particularly African Ameri-

Though mining, farming, and logging are in decline, tourism has recently become a new industry in the mountains.

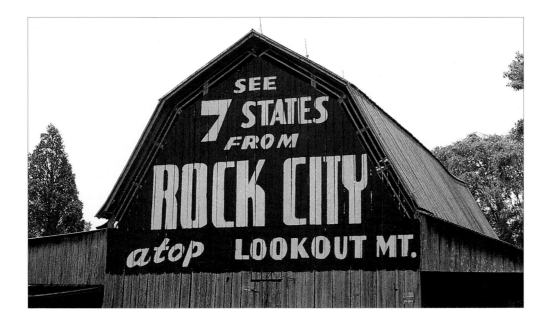

cans, had to move to northern cities such as Detroit to work in factories, or were forced onto government assistance if they wanted to remain in the mountains. Most found that they couldn't return to farming. The thin soil was either exhausted or simply gone, eroded by rains washing down clear-cut mountainsides. More critically, the people themselves had changed. Many had lost the knowledge and skills they needed to make a living on subsistence farms.

The resulting deep poverty of Appalachia was ignored for many years but was "discovered" in 1961, when John F. Kennedy visited the region during his presidential campaign. He couldn't believe that so many poor people could be hidden in the hills and hollows so near the properous eastern seaboard. After his election, he created the National Advisory Commission on Rural Poverty, which determined that "most of the rural South is one vast poverty area." Attention was again focused on the region in 1965, when President Lyndon Johnson provided federal funds through the Appalachian Regional Development Act, which created a program to assist poor mountain people. He hoped to create a Great Society of "abundance and liberty for all." Unfortunately, the program did little, if anything, to help people in the mountains.

Today many people continue to leave the mountains in search of a better life elsewhere. Many of the remaining people have abandoned the traditional

Hidden away in the mountains and valleys, many Appalachian people continue to live in stark poverty. In these isolated pockets, far from urban centers, they still go unnoticed from one generation to the next.

way of life. They now shop for groceries and clothing at the modern stores that have popped up in cities and towns. Rather than provide for themselves, they "live out of bags." Yet there are pockets

way back in the hills where people live as they did a hundred years ago.

However, there is more to Appalachian culture than living off the land. The importance of tradition and kin, the love of storytelling and music, and the ability to work with one's hands are all part of mountain life. People have begun to look back at the old ways, not only to remember them but to keep them alive. Bruce Greene, a mountain musician from Celo, North Carolina, says, "The music is especially threatened. You can't look in an old barn and find it the way you can find an old plow or piece of harness. The music must be passed down from generation to generation."

Despite problems and misconceptions, the spirit

There's an underlying sense of peace and tranquillity along the quiet mountain roads, whether one is resting on the porch or working out in the barn. (Opposite: courtesy Warren Brunner)

of Appalachia—as a people and a place—flourishes today. Shimmering new highways wind their way through mountains and valleys, so the region is no longer isolated—at least, not as much as in the past. People have also embraced modern technology such as computers, along with fast-food chains and other potentially less desirable features of modern life. Folks tend to have a deep regard for education, yet their idea of knowledge includes their own history and distinctive culture. To this very day, along with these new features, a timeless feeling persists throughout Appalachia, captured both in the high peaks and in the homesteads nestled deep in the wooded valleys.

Further Reading

Excellent articles about Appalachia may be found in the *World Book Encyclopedia, Academic American Encyclopedia,* and *Encyclopedia Americana,* all of which were consulted in the research for this book. The *Encyclopedia of Southern Culture* proved to be an invaluable source of information on Appalachia.

Numerous books about Appalachia have also been published for those who would like to read more about this fascinating region. *Appalachian Values,* with text by Loyal Jones and photographs by Warren Brunner, is an especially good book. All of the following books were consulted in the preparation of *Mist Over the Mountains:*

Carson, Jo. *Stories I Ain't Told Nobody Yet: Selections from the People Pieces.* New York: Orchard Books, 1989.

Caudill, Harry. *Night Comes to the Cumberlands: A Biography of a Depressed Area.* Boston: Little, Brown, 1962.

Farwell, Harold F., Jr., and Nicholas, J. Karl, eds. *Smoky Mountain Voices: A Lexicon of Southern Appalachian Speech Based on the Research of Horace Kephart.* Lexington: University Press of Kentucky, 1993.

Goodrich, Frances Louisa. *Mountain Homespun.* New Haven: Yale University Press, 1931.

Joslin, Michael, and Joslin, Ruth. *Mountain People, Places and Ways: A Southern Appalachian Sampler.* Johnson City, Tenn.: Overmountain Press, 1991.

Jones, Loyal. *Appalachian Values*. Ashland, Ky.: Jesse Stuart Foundation, 1994.

Jones, Loyal, and Wheeler, Billy Edd, eds. *Curing the Cross-Eyed Mule: Appalachian Mountain Humor*. Little Rock, Ark.: August House, 1989.

———. *Laughter in Appalachia*. Little Rock, Ark.: August House, 1987.

Rice, Otis. *The Hatfields and the McCoys*. Lexington: University Press of Kentucky, 1982.

Shackelford, Laurel, and Weinberg, Bill, eds. *Our Appalachia*. New York: Hill and Wang, 1977.

Still, James. *The Wolfpen Notebooks: A Record of Appalachian Life*. Lexington: University Press of Kentucky, 1991.

Thomas, Roy Edwin. *Come Go with Me: Old-time Stories from the Southern Mountains*. New York: Farrar, Straus, & Giroux, 1994.

Waller, Altina L. *Feud: Hatfields, McCoys, and Social Change in Appalachia, 1860-1900*. Chapel Hill: University of North Carolina Press, 1988.

Williamson, J. W., and Arnold, Edwin T. *Interviewing Appalachia: The Appalachian Journal Interviews, 1978-1992*. Knoxville: University of Tennessee Press, 1994.